CAREERS MAKING A DIFFERENCE

HELPING THOSE WITH MENTAL ILLNESSES

CAREERS MAKING A DIFFERENCE

HELPING ANIMALS

HELPING CHILDREN

HELPING SENIORS

HELPING THOSE IN POVERTY

HELPING THOSE WITH ADDICTIONS

HELPING THOSE WITH DISABILITIES

HELPING THOSE WITH MENTAL ILLNESSES

HELPING TO PROTECT THE ENVIRONMENT

HELPING VICTIMS

CAREERS MAKING A DIFFERENCE

HELPING THOSE WITH MENTAL ILLNESSES

AMANDA TURNER

MASON CREST

PHILADELPHIA
MIAMI

MASON CREST
450 Parkway Drive, Suite D, Broomall, Pennsylvania 19008
(866) MCP-BOOK (toll-free) • www.masoncrest.com

Printed in the United States of America

First printing
9 8 7 6 5 4 3 2 1

ISBN (hardback) 978-1-4222-4260-5
ISBN (series) 978-1-4222-4253-7
ISBN (ebook) 978-1-4222-7546-7

Cataloging-in-Publication Data on file with the Library of Congress

NATIONAL HIGHLIGHTS

Developed and produced by National Highlights Inc.
Editor: Susan Uttendorfsky
Interior and cover design: Torque Advertising + Design
Production: Michelle Luke

TABLE OF CONTENTS

KEY ICONS TO LOOK FOR

Words to Understand: These words with their easy-to-understand definitions will increase the reader's understanding of the text while building vocabulary skills.

Sidebars: This boxed material within the main text allows readers to build knowledge, gain insights, explore possibilities, and broaden their perspectives by weaving together additional information to provide realistic and holistic perspectives.

Educational Videos: Readers can view videos by scanning our QR codes, providing them with additional educational content to supplement the text. Examples include news coverage, moments in history, speeches, iconic sports moments, and much more!

Text-Dependent Questions: These questions send the reader back to the text for more careful attention to the evidence presented there.

Research Projects: Readers are pointed toward areas of further inquiry connected to each chapter. Suggestions are provided for projects that encourage deeper research and analysis.

Series Glossary of Key Terms: This back-of-the-book glossary contains terminology used throughout this series. Words found here increase the reader's ability to read and comprehend higher-level books and articles in this field.

AWARENESS OF THE CAUSE

Mental illness is prevalent in the United States today. It is considered to be a major public health issue that affects twenty percent of adults. However, the real numbers of those suffering is likely to be much higher. People with a mental illness often feel uncomfortable or afraid of seeking help. They feel that if their work colleagues or friends find out about their condition, they will be judged negatively. Fortunately, society is becoming more accepting of the many types of mental illnesses and their treatments.

"People become attached to their burdens sometimes more than the burdens are attached to them."
– George Bernard Shaw

"There is nothing either good or bad, but thinking makes it so."
– William Shakespeare

"Depression is being colorblind and constantly told how colorful the world is."
– Atticus

"Mental pain is less dramatic than physical pain, but it is more common and also more hard to bear."
– C.S. Lewis

CHAPTER 1

Is a Career in Mental Health For You?

Most people have a worthy cause that they believe in. You can even work in this field yourself by following a career and making a difference to those in need.

- Start out as a volunteer.
- Seek out a personal connection in the field.
- Develop an inspirational mission statement for yourself.
- Find out about the education, training, and qualifications required for your chosen career.
- Study job specifications of interest.
- Discuss your goals with your loved ones.
- Approach school counselors, charities, and organizations to obtain advice.

MENTAL HEALTH STATISTICS

Approximately 1 in 5 adults in the United States— 43.8 million, or 18.5%—experiences a mental illness in a given year.

MENTAL ILLNESSES: CHILDREN

Approximately 1 in 5 young people aged 13–18 (21.4%) experiences a severe mental disorder at some point during their life. For children aged 8–15, the estimate is 13%.

- **Suicide is the 10th leading cause of death in the United States, and the second leading cause of death for people aged 10–34.**

- **Half of all chronic mental illness begins by age 14 and three-quarters by age 24. Despite effective treatment, there are often long delays between the first appearance of symptoms and when people eventually get help.**

TREATMENT FOR YOUTH DEPRESSION

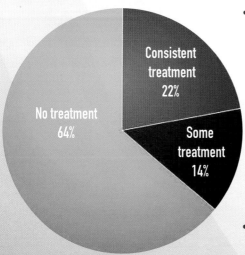

Consistent treatment 22%

No treatment 64%

Some treatment 14%

Source: Mental Health America.

MENTAL ILLNESSES: ADULTS

- **Only 41% of adults in the United States with a mental health condition received mental health services in the past year. Among adults with a serious mental illness, 62.9% received mental health services in the past year.**

- **Serious mental illness costs America $193.2 billion in lost earnings per year.**

- **Each day an estimated 18–22 veterans die by suicide.**

Source: National Alliance of Mental Illnesses.

MENTAL ILLNESSES: SOCIETY

Approximately 1 in 25 adults in the U.S.—9.8 million, or 4.0%—experiences a serious mental illness in a given year that substantially interferes with or limits one or more major life activities.

- **An estimated 26% of homeless adults staying in shelters live with serious mental illness, and an estimated 46% live with severe mental illness and/or substance use disorders.**

- **Approximately 20% of state prisoners and 21% of local jail prisoners have a recent history of a mental health condition.**

- **70% of youth in juvenile justice systems have at least one mental health condition, and at least 20% live with a serious mental illness.**

- **18.1% of adults in the U.S. experienced an anxiety disorder such as posttraumatic stress disorder, obsessive-compulsive disorder, and specific phobias.**

Source: www.nimh.nih.gov.

MOST COMMON MENTAL ILLNESSES IN THE U.S.

- Major depression
- Personality disorders
- Bipolar disorder
- Attention-deficit/ hyperactivity disorder (ADHD)
- Autism spectrum disorder (ASD)
- Schizophrenia
- Personality disorders
- Posttraumatic stress disorder (PTSD)
- Obsessive-compulsive disorder (OCD)
- Suicide
- Eating disorders
- Phobias

Source: National Institute of Mental Health.

DID YOU KNOW?

- **People with mental illnesses often feel afraid to seek help.**

- **Stigma and discrimination can also worsen a mental illness.**

- **Most people who experience mental health problems recover fully or are able to live with and manage them.**

AWARENESS OF THE CAUSE

6 Counselor

1 Hotlines & Helplines

5 Mental Health Services

WHERE DO THOSE WITH MENTAL ILLNESSES SEEK HELP?

2 Mental Health Charities

4 Therapist

3 Support Organizations

WHAT SHOULD A MENTALLY ILL PERSON DO TO GET HELP?

- Seek understanding and sympathy
- Find information about where to get treatment or therapy

- Seek help from loved ones
- Find out information about mental illnesses and types of treatment available
- Do not delay seeking help

THE BENEFITS OF HELPING OTHERS

A SENSE OF PURPOSE
Giving to others provides a sense of purpose to an individual. People who volunteer for a cause feel that their life is worthwhile and satisfying. This ultimately leads to improved physical and emotional health.

EMOTIONAL HEALTH
Studies have also shown that the act of charity results in emotional well-being. The person who gives to charity feels improved self-esteem. This gives a feeling of satisfaction to the individual. In a way, giving to others allows the individual to create a "kindness bank account." The more kind acts are filled in the account, the better the emotional state of the person.

A HEALTHY HEART
A recent study found that there is a significant correlation between helping others and the heart's health. It was found that people who volunteer are about 40 percent less likely to develop high blood pressure as compared to those who do not volunteer.

HELPING OTHERS MAKES YOU HAPPY
According to research, people who engage in acts of kindness and giving are happier in general as compared to others. Acts of kindness carried out regularly or even once a week can lead to greater happiness and joy in life.

REDUCE STRESS
The act of helping others can also help reduce stress. Research shows that people who help others have lower cortisol levels. The presence of this hormone in the body creates feelings of anxiety and panic, which can lead to higher blood pressure levels. People who do less for others have a higher level of the stress hormone in their body.

Milestone Moment

PUBLICATION OF DR. SIGMUND FREUD'S
THE INTERPRETATION OF DREAMS, 1900

Dr. Sigmund Freud (1909)

When people hear the name Sigmund Freud, psychology immediately comes to mind. Dr. Freud was one of the first medical professionals to study the mind and how it creates our feelings, thoughts, and behaviors. Freud is regarded as the father of psychotherapy, also known as "talk therapy."

Prior to Freud, those who suffered from mental illnesses were often thought of as crazy. The medical community did not understand that mental illnesses were treatable diseases with real chemical causes. Sometimes the public even thought that mental illness was the result of being cursed or possessed by a demon.

Freud was the first doctor to treat sufferers with talk therapy. Through conversation, Freud believed that he could help people uncover deep-rooted issues that were contributing to their mental illness. His first book, *The Interpretation of Dreams*, suggested that there was much more going on in the mind than anyone had previously realized. Freud theorized that we have a subconscious mind that influences our dreams and our behaviors.

While many of Freud's ideas have since been disproven, talk therapy still remains a common part of the treatment of mental health disorders today.

WORDS TO UNDERSTAND

binge eating: the consumption of extremely large amounts of food in a short period of time; usually a symptom of disordered eating

continuum: the continuous sequence, ranging from inconsequential to extreme, on which most mental illnesses are viewed by mental health professionals

stigma: a physical or unseen social mark of disgrace associated with a particular condition

suicide: the act of taking one's own life

CHAPTER 2

Helping Those with Mental Illnesses: Why It's Needed

EXPLORING THE HUMAN MIND

The mind is fascinating. In recent years, modern medicine has made great strides in understanding how the brain works, and there is still much to be discovered. The field of psychology is always evolving. Once thought of as a pseudoscience, the study of psychology is now well respected in the fields of medicine, education, and social work.

A part of psychology is the study of mental illness. There are different categories of mental illness, including depression, anxiety disorders, addiction issues, and personality disorders. There are varied careers available for people who want to work with those suffering from mental illness.

IF SOMEONE IS SAD, DOES THAT MEAN THEY ARE DEPRESSED?

This can be a tricky question to answer. It's normal to go through periods of sadness, especially during a difficult life event, such as a breakup, a death in the family, a job loss, etc. Sometimes individuals feel sad for no reason at all. When someone is clinically depressed, it usually lasts longer than typical sadness—more than six weeks. It's usually accompanied by changes in eating or sleeping habits, a loss of interest in usual activities, and a feeling of hopelessness. If you're worried that you or a friend might be depressed, it's a good idea to talk to a school counselor.

One in five adults in the United States suffers from a mental illness. It's likely that this number is even higher, as a lot of sufferers unfortunately do not seek medical treatment. While treatment is widely available, only 44 percent of Americans see a doctor or therapist for mental health treatment. As time goes on, the **stigma** attached to seeking treatment for mental health issues continues to dissipate. People who have mental health issues are becoming more comfortable coming forward due to public acceptance of mental illness as a legitimate disease. As more individuals seek help for mental health issues, the need for mental health professionals increases.

Since mental illness is so prevalent in the United States today, there are many different opportunities for careers in the field. In order to have a successful career in a mental health profession, it's important to learn about the different mental illnesses from which people suffer. While it's impossible to fully understand someone's personal experience with mental illness, knowing the symptoms typically associated with each type of illness can help provide a basic idea of what the disorder is like.

Along with understanding the different types of mental illness, mental health professionals need to have training in how to listen effectively, how to help someone share their feelings and experiences without feeling judged, and how to develop a treatment plan to help an individual work through their mental illness.

In contrast to those with physical illnesses, people who have mental health issues are often reluctant to come forward to seek help.

While mental illness may not present with physical symptoms like other diseases, those who are suffering from mental health issues need medical and/or psychological treatment. This can mean medication administered in a mental health facility or hospital, medication prescribed by a psychiatrist, therapy with a psychologist or counselor, lifestyle changes, or a combination of all of these approaches. The descriptions below explain some of the symptoms associated with different types of mental illness.

All mental illnesses exist on a **continuum**. This means that various individuals who suffer from the same mental illness will have different symptoms and varying levels of severity of those symptoms. The degree to which someone is suffering from a mental illness can help determine the level of treatment that they need. Someone who struggles with occasional bouts of depression may be able to work through their issues with talk therapy, while someone who has been clinically depressed for years and struggles with suicidal thoughts may require more intense treatment.

Students who study subjects relating to mental health learn about all the different kinds of illnesses including depression, anxiety, addiction issues, and personality disorders.

The criteria for what constitutes a mental illness is constantly changing. Mental health professionals rely on a guide called the *DSM*, which stands for the *Diagnostic and Statistical Manual to Mental Disorders*. The *DSM* is updated regularly by the American Psychiatric Association.

TYPES OF MENTAL ILLNESS
ANXIETY AND PANIC ATTACKS

Anxiety is a feeling of uneasiness or discomfort related to being nervous. Everyone experiences anxiety at some point

The human mind has always been the subject of fascination. In recent years, scientists have made great progress in understanding how our brains work.

in their lives, and for most people, this is normal. Anxiety might arise before taking a test or before asking someone out on a date. It is often referred to as a "butterflies in the stomach" feeling. Anxiety often builds as the event nears. Then the anxiety-causing event happens, and the anxiety goes away. For people with anxiety disorders, things work a little bit differently. The anxiety doesn't leave after the event, and sometimes, the anxiety appears without an event at all.

There are different types of anxiety disorders. Panic attacks are when anxiety presents with severe physical symptoms, such as shortness of breath, chest pains, gastrointestinal upset, flushed skin, shaking, and dizziness. Sometimes those experiencing panic attacks feel that they may be having a heart attack or that they are dying. Anxiety and panic issues can be treated with a talk therapy and/or medication.

BIPOLAR DISORDER

Bipolar disorder is one of the most commonly misunderstood mental illnesses. The public generally believes that people who are bipolar experience extreme mood swings and are constantly switching from one mood to the next. This is not actually what most bipolar patients experience. There are two parts to bipolar disorder: depression and mania. Persons with the disorder generally experience mania, also known as a "manic state," for a few days at a time. During these days, they typically engage in reckless behavior, such as drinking, using drugs, spending

A person suffering from bipolar disorder may have periods when they experience mania followed by periods of depression.

lots of money, and engaging in sexual behavior that is unusual for them. This is followed by a depressive period when they often withdraw, feel very sad, and may even become suicidal. Depressive periods can last anywhere from a few weeks to a few months.

Bipolar disorder is usually treated with medication and talk therapy. Sometimes successful treatment for manic or depressive episodes requires hospital admission.

BODY DYSMORPHIC DISORDER

For most individuals, looking in the mirror is an accurate reflection of reality. This is not the case for a person with body dysmorphia. When someone with this illness looks in the mirror, they see a negatively skewed version of their body. Sometimes they see themselves as overweight when

Body dysmorphia is a mental illness that manifests itself when a person looks in a mirror and sees a negatively skewed version of themselves.

they are actually at a healthy weight. They may fixate on certain parts of their body, such as their nose or their teeth.

Some people who suffer from body dysmorphic disorder have plastic surgery to fix their perceived flaws, but no matter how many surgeries they have, they are still not happy with how they look. Patients with body dysmorphia often become obsessed with their looks, and they believe that others are obsessed with their looks as well. They are often very self-conscious and struggle to go about normal daily activities.

Body dysmorphic disorder is typically treated with talk therapy.

PERSONALITY DISORDERS

Personality disorders are long-term mental illnesses that typically leave a person struggling to maintain healthy relationships (with employers, significant others, family, etc.). There are ten different personality disorders, broken down into three categories, also known as "clusters": suspicious, emotional/impulsive, and anxious.

The suspicious cluster includes schizotypal, schizoid, and paranoid personality disorders. These are grouped together because they all involve odd or eccentric behavior. People who have a disorder in this cluster often struggle with homelessness, drug addiction, and alcohol issues.

The emotional/impulsive cluster includes antisocial, borderline, histrionic, and narcissistic personality disorders. These disorders are grouped together because they involve dramatic, emotional, or erratic behavior. Sufferers from an illness in the emotional/ impulsive cluster often find themselves having great

Those who suffer from a personality disorder often struggle with their everyday lives. They may have problems forming relationships and find work life challenging.

difficulty maintaining successful romantic relationships and/or calm family relationships.

The anxious cluster includes avoidant, dependent, and obsessive-compulsive personality disorders (obsessive-compulsive personality disorder is different from obsessive-compulsive disorder). Most people who have disorders in this area struggle to have success at work or at school. Sufferers in this category sometimes have trouble getting work done because they do not want to start until they know exactly how to do the work perfectly. The fear of making a mistake can stop them from getting started. These personality disorders are grouped together because they involve anxious or fearful behaviors.

Personality disorders are typically treated with a combination of medication and talk therapy.

MAJOR DEPRESSIVE DISORDER

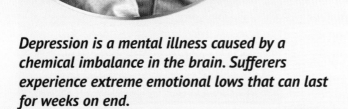

Some individuals think that depression is just feeling sad, but it's much more serious than that. When someone is depressed enough to warrant a psychological diagnosis, they don't just feel down. They have extreme emotional lows that last for weeks. These emotional lows are often accompanied by changes in appetite, changes in sleep, loss of interest in usual

Depression is a mental illness caused by a chemical imbalance in the brain. Sufferers experience extreme emotional lows that can last for weeks on end.

Unfortunately, mental illnesses are common in the United States with at least twenty percent of adults suffering at some stage of their lives. Some illnesses can even lead to thoughts of suicide.

activities, a sense of hopelessness, and, sometimes, suicidal thoughts.

Major depressive disorder is actually caused by a chemical imbalance in the brain, much like strep throat is caused by bacteria or like a stomach flu is caused by a virus. Clinical depression is a real chemical problem, and it's not possible for someone who is dealing with it to simply "snap out of it."

Clinical depression is treatable and does not have to last a lifetime. Some people find success treating depression with holistic methods, and some find success using a combination of psychotherapy and antidepressant medications.

Depression is an illness that can be treated, usually by using a combination of medication and psychotherapy prescribed by a qualified mental health professional.

DRUG AND ALCOHOL ADDICTION

There has been a change in the psychology world over the past few decades when it comes to people who struggle with addiction. Addiction to drugs and alcohol is now recognized as a disease of the brain rather than just a lack of willpower. When some folks use drugs and alcohol, their brains create unique chemical pathways that leave them more susceptible to addiction than other people. Neurologists and psychologists are not completely sure why this happens to some individuals and not others, but it's likely due to a combination of environmental and biological factors.

Certain genetic factors and life stressors can both contribute to a person's struggle with addiction. Some people who suffer from addiction are also suffering from another mental health condition. When someone suffers from both addiction and a separate mental illness, they are referred to as a

For many years, dependence on drugs and alcohol was considered to be caused by a lack of willpower. However, more recently, this type of addiction is now recognized as a disease of the brain.

"dual-diagnosis patient." Those who suffer from addiction can find success with a combination of medication and talk therapy, as well as participation in group therapy, such as Alcoholics Anonymous.

EATING DISORDERS

While there are many types of eating disorders, the three most common are anorexia nervosa, bulimia nervosa, and OSFED, which stands for other specified feeding or eating disorder. Commonly, people suffering from eating disorders are deeply anxious and want to have strict control over certain areas of their lives, such as choosing exactly what food to eat and/or how much to exercise. Folks who have eating disorders engage in this behavior to the extreme, and it affects their well-being.

Individuals who are anorexic have a significantly low body weight and feel as though they are never thin enough. Those

People with anorexia nervosa deny their body of adequate nutrition and often exercise obsessively to keep their weight down.

who are bulimic go through episodes of **binge eating** and then use unhealthy methods in an attempt to quickly get rid of what they ate, such as excessive exercise or self-induced vomiting.

People with OSFED do not fit neatly into one of these boxes, but they

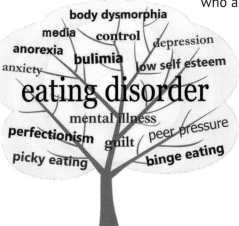

There are three common types of eating disorder: anorexia nervosa, bulimia nervosa, and OSFED, which stands other specified feeding or eating disorder.

Obsessive-compulsive disorder (OCD) sufferers can sometimes fear germs, leading to repeated handwashing.

have eating habits that are not conducive to good health, and they are dissatisfied with their bodies to the point where it creates a severe disruption in their everyday life.

Eating disorder recovery can take a long time, but many successfully go through therapy and learn how to create a positive relationship with food.

OBSESSIVE-COMPULSIVE DISORDER

It's common to hear people say that they have OCD, meaning that they like to keep things neat and organized. Actual obsessive-compulsive disorder is much more complicated. OCD is comprised of two parts. There are obsessions, which are intrusive, unwanted thoughts. These thoughts can come rapidly and seemingly without reason. Some OCD sufferers experience intrusive thoughts from

Some OCD sufferers can be anxious about making everything look orderly.

the moment they wake up in the morning until the moment they fall asleep at night.

The other part of OCD is compulsions, which are behaviors that the person with OCD feels compelled to do because of the obsessive thoughts. Often, the obsessions and compulsions are seemingly unrelated. For example, someone with OCD might feel the need to touch a light switch a certain number of times so that no one in their family is hurt in a car accident.

A person with OCD has a chemical imbalance that makes it hard for the brain to separate rational behavior from irrational behavior, especially when it's related to anxiety. People who have OCD typically find relief with a combination of talk therapy and medication.

PHOBIAS

A phobia is the clinical term for an extreme or irrational fear. Some phobias are common, such as aviophobia—the fear of flying. Others are more obscure, such as myrmecophobia, the fear of ants. For some, their phobia is not something that they have to deal with in everyday life, so they may

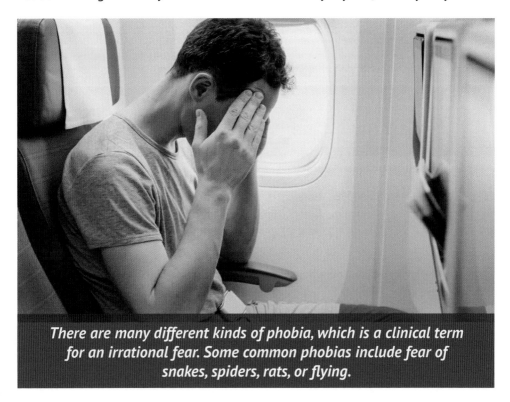

There are many different kinds of phobia, which is a clinical term for an irrational fear. Some common phobias include fear of snakes, spiders, rats, or flying.

choose not to treat it. For other people, a phobia may keep them from accomplishing their typical activities of daily living. In these cases, it's important for people suffering from phobias to seek treatment.

Patients who suffer from severe phobias frequently find success with cognitive behavioral therapy. This type of therapy helps change the thought patterns and behaviors related to their phobia.

POSTTRAUMATIC STRESS DISORDER

Posttraumatic stress disorder, or PTSD, is a condition that some people experience after a dangerous, scary, or shocking event. In movies, we often see characters experience PTSD after military service. While it is certainly possible for someone to experience PTSD after serving in a war, there are many other situations that can result in this disorder as well.

During dangerous or scary situations, it's normal for the body to go into "fight or flight" mode. During fight or flight mode, the body releases adrenaline and prepares the body to protect itself if necessary. This surge of adrenaline provides the body with the energy it needs to either fight off an attacker or flee from an attacker.

For most people, these chemical changes go away after the event ends. For individuals with PTSD, they continue to experience reactions to trauma even after the trauma has happened. People who have PTSD may experience flashbacks (seeing the event in their mind even though it is no longer happening), an inability to remember key details of the

Posttraumatic stress disorder can manifest itself due to a number of reasons. PTSD is a mental illness often associated with soldiers returning from the front line.

Premenstrual dysphoric disorder, or PMDD, is a severe form of premenstrual syndrome.

traumatic event, nightmares, scary thoughts, and a desire to avoid others or places that remind them of the traumatic event. They may become so stressed that they have angry outbursts or regularly feel tense or on edge. They may also experience some depression-like symptoms, such as a loss of enjoyment in activities they used to like or negative thoughts about the world and themselves.

Not everyone who experiences a traumatic event will develop PTSD. Psychologists are not completely sure why some people develop PTSD while others do not. A combination of medication and talk therapy is the current go-to treatment for patients who are suffering from PTSD.

PREMENSTRUAL DYSPHORIC DISORDER

Premenstrual dysphoric disorder, or PMDD, is a severe form of PMS, or premenstrual syndrome. When women experience PMS, they often have food cravings, mood swings, fatigue, and cramps, and these symptoms generally happen about a week or so before their menstrual period begins.

Women who suffer from PMDD experience these symptoms to an extreme degree and find that their symptoms are debilitating to the point where they are unable to participate in their normal work or school activities.

This can make it hard to be successful at work or school and can cause issues with relationships.

PMDD sufferers may also experience anxiety, feelings of hopelessness, hot flashes, joint pain, and intense feelings of anger or hostility toward other individuals. Doctors aren't sure why some women experience PMDD and others do not. Usually, PMDD is treated with hormonal therapy or other medication.

SCHIZOPHRENIA

Schizophrenia is not as common as it is portrayed in the media. Schizophrenia affects how a person thinks, feels, and behaves, and it presents differently in each person. Some of those who are schizophrenic suffer from mental issues that may make it appear that they are out of touch with reality.

People with schizophrenia may experience auditory and/or visual hallucinations. Other symptoms are varied. Sufferers can find social interaction difficult and become withdrawn.

People with this disease may experience auditory and/or visual hallucinations, dysfunctional ways of thinking, paranoia, agitated body movements, reduced speaking, withdrawal from regular daily activities, and a flat affect (reduced facial expressions, monotone voice).

Not everyone who suffers from one or some of these symptoms has schizophrenia, and patients with schizophrenia rarely suffer from all of these issues at one time. Schizophrenia is typically treated with a combination of medication and talk therapy. Sometimes hospitalization is required for those who suffer from schizophrenia.

Light therapy is sometimes prescribed to people with SAD. SAD is a mental illness that strikes in the winter months and causes depression. It is thought that it may be caused by a lack of vitamin D.

SEASONAL AFFECTIVE DISORDER

Seasonal affective disorder, or SAD, is a specific type of depression that strikes in the winter months. It's thought that this may be caused by a lack of vitamin D. The body typically produces vitamin D when exposed to the sun. The lack of sunlight during the winter months, especially in the Northern Hemisphere, may contribute to a chemical imbalance, resulting in seasonal depression.

Some people have success treating SAD by using light therapy lamps to help their body produce vitamin D. Patients who suffer from SAD may also see success through a combination of talk therapy and medication.

SELF-INJURY DISORDER

People who have self-injury disorder intentionally cause harm to their bodies. Typically this is done by cutting, burning, pulling out hair, picking at the skin excessively, and picking at cuts. These injuries are repeated to the point where they leave lasting marks or scars. Self-injury disorder is most common in individuals who lack a support system to help them cope with stress. People who have obsessive-compulsive disorder, anxiety disorders, and depression are more likely to engage in self-injury than those who do not have these illnesses.

While self-injury disorder can be classified as a mental illness

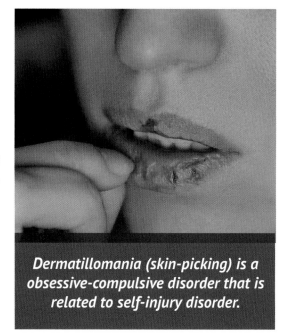

Dermatillomania (skin-picking) is a obsessive-compulsive disorder that is related to self-injury disorder.

Self-injury may take many forms such as cutting or even burning the skin.

on its own, usually individuals who suffer from self-injuring behaviors also have another mental illness. Those who deliberately self-harm often find relief with a treatment combination of talk therapy and medication.

SUICIDAL FEELINGS

Each year, 9.6 million people in the United States have suicidal thoughts. This does not necessarily mean that they have attempted **suicide**, but it does mean that they are more likely to head down that path than someone who has not had suicidal thoughts in

There are many reasons why a person may have suicidal thoughts. People who experience them may be suffering from a traumatic life event or mental illness. Suicidal people should seek help from a counselor, teacher, or a trusted adult immediately.

the past. Suicidal thoughts are sometimes situational, meaning they follow a significant (and often traumatic) life event, such as a job loss, loss of a relationship, a death in the family, or serious financial trouble. Having suicidal thoughts does not mean a person will be thought of as crazy or admitted to a hospital. It may simply mean that they need someone to talk to.

If you are experiencing suicidal thoughts, talk to a counselor or teacher right away. If you're not comfortable doing that, call the National Suicide Hotline at 1-800-273-8255. Calls to the hotline are confidential and are handled by a trained crisis counselor who will be able to help.

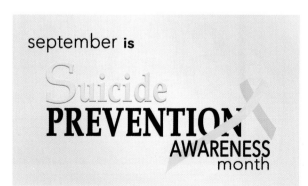

september **is**

Suicide
PREVENTION
AWARENESS
month

A DAY IN THE LIFE: ADDICTION COUNSELOR

An addiction counselor has many different aspects to their job in helping their clients get the help that they need. Addiction counselors often start their day by doing intake interviews for new patients who are checking into detox or rehab to start their journey toward getting help. After that, addiction counselors may have one-on-one therapy sessions, lead group therapy sessions, and help people develop after-care plans to help them continue their journey toward staying clean after they leave the facility.

Addiction counselors also spend part of their day contacting halfway houses, shelters, and housing management offices to help find appropriate places for their patients to live after they leave their care.

WHAT IS SCHIZOPHRENIA?

Watch this video to learn about the different types of schizophrenia and to gain a deeper understanding about what life is like for a person suffering from this disease

TEXT-DEPENDENT QUESTIONS

1. What are the symptoms of posttraumatic stress disorder?

2. What are the three main classifications of eating disorders?

3. What are the three clusters of personality disorders?

RESEARCH PROJECT

Choose one of the mental illnesses listed above, and research how treatment for this disorder has changed throughout history. Be sure to include how outcomes for patients have changed as treatments became, and continue to become, more advanced.

NATIONAL MENTAL HEALTH ACT—JULY 3, 1946

The signing of the National Mental Health Act allowed funds to be allotted to form the National Institute of Mental Health (NIMH). The formation of NIMH then provided funding for the treatment of mental illness in the United States. This was hugely important because up until this point, the quality of care in mental health facilities was abysmal. Patients were often treated inhumanely, given abusive treatments, and neglected for long periods of time. Mental health facilities were typically similar to high-security jails, with patients being locked in their rooms for days at a time.

The National Mental Health Act allowed mental health professionals to conduct research and learn that most people suffering from mental health issues have a better chance at recovery when they are only briefly hospitalized or treated on an outpatient basis, rather than being institutionalized. In addition, the new drugs and treatment methods that resulted from the National Mental Health Act improved the lives of millions of patients suffering from mental health issues.

HELPING THOSE WITH MENTAL ILLNESSES

WORDS TO UNDERSTAND

confidential: private

crisis: a time of intense difficulty or trouble

de-escalate: reducing the intensity of a violent or potentially violent situation

HIPAA: the Health Insurance Portability and Accountability Act, which protects private health information

institutionalized: the process of long-term (sometimes lifelong) housing in a mental health facility due to mental illness

CHAPTER 3

Volunteering and Organizations

BECOMING A MENTAL HEALTH VOLUNTEER

Thinking about volunteering to help those suffering from mental health issues? Volunteering is a great way to find out if a career in mental health might be a good fit for you. Due to confidentiality laws, many mental health facilities only allow volunteers who are over the age of eighteen and trained in **HIPAA** regulations. If you are not yet eighteen years old, talk to your guidance counselor about opportunities at your school to help struggling students. This might be an easier place to start, rather than approaching a mental health facility.

Volunteering with mental health patients can feel a little bit scary at first. It's normal to feel nervous, but it's important to remember that individuals who suffer from mental illness are still just regular people. Treat the patients you interact with the same as you would treat any other acquaintance. Get to know them as a person, not as the face of a disorder.

You'll need to build trust with the patients you work with before they feel comfortable opening up to you. This can take time and patience. Your volunteer supervisor will be able to help you practice trust-building techniques to help patients get to know you.

Before you interact with patients, you'll go through training with a supervisor. You may be asked to role-play as if you are interacting with a patient. While this might feel silly at first, it's one of the best ways to practice the work you'll actually be doing. During training, don't be afraid to ask questions to ensure that you fully understand your role as a volunteer.

Volunteering with mental health patients is a very rewarding experience. You will need to build trust with patients so that they feel comfortable in your company.

CONFIDENTIALITY

Even as a volunteer, it's imperative that you keep the information shared by the folks you help **confidential**. This means that everything the people you work with tell you must stay private—just between you and them. While this shows respect for the patient, it's also a legal issue. There are laws in place, like HIPAA, that protect patient privacy.

There are a few exceptions to this rule:

• If the person you are working with tells you that they are thinking about

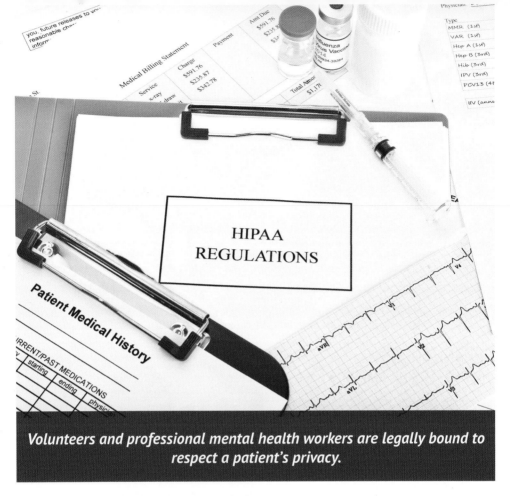

Text on image:
- you, future releases to...reasonable cha... inform...
- Medical Billing Statement
- Payment
- Amt Due $591.76 $235.87 $34...
- Service X-ray ...draw
- Charge $591.76 $235.87 $342.78
- Total Amo... $1.17...
- fluenza Virus Vaccine 934-302#4
- Physician...
- Type MMR (1st) VAR (1st) Hep A (1st) Hep B (3rd) Hib (3rd) IPV (3rd) PCV13 (4t... IIV (annu...
- HIPAA REGULATIONS
- Patient Medical History
- ...RRENT/PAST MEDICATIONS starting ending physic...

Volunteers and professional mental health workers are legally bound to respect a patient's privacy.

harming themselves or others, it's critical that you talk to your supervisor. Your supervisor will be able to help you figure out what steps to take next.

- If you suspect that neglect or abuse is happening in the life of the person you are working with, or if you are concerned that they are neglecting or abusing someone else, it's also essential to alert your supervisor.

While these situations are difficult, a good mental health worker always puts the safety of others as their top priority.

It's a good idea to have a conversation with your supervisor about how they'd like you to handle these situations if/when they arise. Some supervisors want volunteers to inform the patients that they must report the information, while other supervisors prefer to talk with the patient one-on-one to determine if there is a safety issue.

HELP! A FRIEND TOLD ME THEY'RE THINKING ABOUT HURTING THEMSELVES.

When people know that you volunteer to help those who are struggling with mental illness, they will often come to you when they are going through their own struggles. This sometimes means that friends or family might want your help during a difficult time. If a friend or a family member tells you that they're thinking about hurting themselves or someone else, talk to a trusted adult, teacher, or guidance counselor right away, even if your friend asked you not to tell anyone. By doing this, you may be saving their life.

ORGANIZATIONS
VOLUNTEERS OF AMERICA

Volunteers of America is an organization that assists individuals who are struggling get back on their feet. A lot of the people who are helped by Volunteers of America are current or former mental health patients. Often, those who deal with homelessness and addiction are also dealing with underlying mental health issues such as bipolar disorder or schizophrenia.

As a volunteer with Volunteers of America, there are a number of ways that you can affect the life of someone suffering from mental illness. You might help them find housing or a job, help them practice interview skills, or simply provide a listening ear to help

For over a century, Volunteers of America has been helping those in need. It has helped many homeless people who are often struggling with mental health issues.

them through their problems. You also may be tasked with helping people find counseling and mental health resources in your community.

Volunteering with Volunteers of America is also a great way to try out different opportunities to get an idea of which human services career path may be a good fit for you.

SUICIDE PREVENTION HOTLINE

When someone feels suicidal, they are often at the lowest point of their life. They feel that their life is hopeless, and they are unable to go on. There are a number of different situations that can cause someone to have suicidal thoughts: a death in the family, guilt over a lost relationship, panic about

Suicide prevention hotlines connect to people who are feeling suicidal. Specially trained people provide the caller with much needed support and advice. These hotlines are usually open for twenty-four hours a day, seven days a week.

losing a job, or even just a long period of being in a depressed state can all cause someone to consider taking their own life.

In their moment of despair, they need someone to help remind them that things will get better and that life is worth living. They need someone who can talk them through their problem and help them discover potential solutions. This is where suicide prevention hotlines come into play.

Suicide prevention hotlines connect folks who are suicidal with living, breathing volunteers who are available to listen twenty-four hours a day, seven days a week. Being a volunteer for a suicide hotline is a huge responsibility, and it's not something to take lightly. Volunteers undergo special training on how to calm a suicidal person down, how to assess the severity of the situation, and how to get the person medical help if they need it. Suicide hotline volunteers are trained to know when to call law enforcement if necessary to provide immediate assistance to the caller.

If you are interested in one day working with people in **crisis**, going through this kind of training is a good first step to see if you are emotionally up to the task. At the end of your training, you may feel that this type of work is not a good fit for you, and that's ok. Talk with your volunteer supervisor to see if perhaps you can help in another way. While this work is very hard, it's also very important. Suicide hotlines

People who call suicide prevention hotlines are likely to be in a very desperate state. For the person taking the call, it can be a stressful experience. For this reason, helpline volunteers have to undergo special training on how to calm a suicidal person down, how to assess the severity of the situation, and how to get medical help if required.

Volunteering at a suicide prevention hotline can be a challenging occupation. However, these hotlines save thousands of lives each year, so it is a very worthwhile thing to do.

save thousands of lives each year, and many callers spend the rest of their lives grateful that someone was there to talk them through their darkest moments.

While numerous sufferers who call the suicide help line are in fact suicidal, there are also other reasons that they might call. They may not be at the point where they want to hurt themselves, but perhaps they are stuck with a difficult life issue, unsure of where to turn next. Even people who have a solid social support system in their life may not feel comfortable talking to their friends or family about certain personal issues.

Sometimes a stranger can provide a better perspective on a situation than someone who is close to the person. Callers are struggling with issues such as gender identity, family issues, breakups, school problems, financial issues, and other problems, and they simply need to talk to someone who is trained in problem-solving and willing to listen.

Crisis text line volunteers provide crisis help within a few minutes to those who send a text. The person in crisis can text back and forth only sharing the information they feel comfortable in sharing. The volunteer will listen to the person texting and provide them with advice and information on how to feel better and get further help.

CRISIS TEXT LINE

Some individuals feel more comfortable reaching out for help through a text message rather than actually talking to someone on the phone. More and more crisis hotlines are beginning to add a text message option. Crisis text lines require that volunteers are at least eighteen years old. Most text lines also require at least two adult references.

As a crisis text volunteer, you'll need to undergo several hours of training. It's important that you do not go through with training unless you plan on fulfilling a commitment as a volunteer. Training typically costs crisis organizations over $1,000 per volunteer. To recoup that expense, most crisis text centers ask that volunteers sign on for at least a 200 hour commitment, with a minimum of four hours worked per week, after they complete their training.

If you're someone who usually stays up late or gets up early, crisis text volunteer work might be a good fit for you. Most crisis texts are received between the hours of 10 p.m. and 6 a.m., and they require a volunteer to work with the person in crisis immediately.

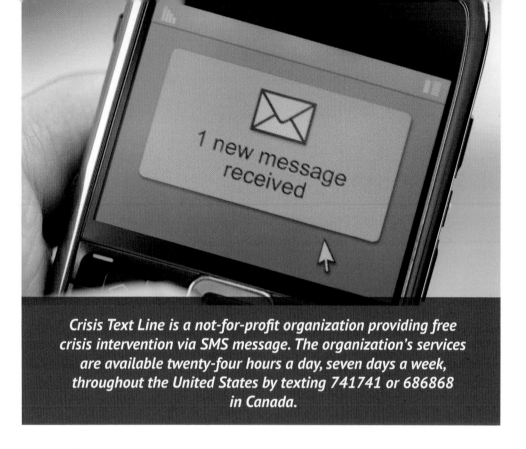

Crisis Text Line is a not-for-profit organization providing free crisis intervention via SMS message. The organization's services are available twenty-four hours a day, seven days a week, throughout the United States by texting 741741 or 686868 in Canada.

While all volunteer commitments are important, people who utilize crisis hotlines are in desperate need of immediate help. It's crucial that you work your shifts without canceling and be dedicated to helping the person on the other end of the phone. You need to give your full attention to the task at hand. This is not work that can be done casually while you're also doing homework or hanging out with friends.

As a text crisis volunteer, much like a suicide hotline volunteer, your first step of working with a texter will be to **de-escalate** the situation. After that, you'll help them work through some constructive problem-solving, as well as creating a safety plan in case they begin to feel like hurting themselves again or hurting someone else.

If you think the field of crisis counseling may be a good fit for you, being a crisis text line volunteer is a wonderful chance to see what the field is actually like. You may feel great satisfaction after helping a caller through a problem. Volunteering with a crisis text line is an excellent advantage on your resume for graduate school as well.

PEER COUNSELING/MEDIATION

Your school may offer a peer counseling program through the guidance office. In peer counseling, students work with other students to talk through personal problems. Peer counselors receive special training to help them develop listening and problem-solving skills.

If you are a nonjudgmental person who is a good listener, peer counseling might be a good fit for you. If your guidance office does not already have a peer counseling program in place, you might talk to your guidance counselors about starting one.

Peer mediation is also a good program for getting started with helping others solve their problems. In peer mediation, two students who are struggling with a disagreement will sign up to meet with you for a session. You'll provide a listening ear and give them potential solutions to help work out their problem. Sometimes students find it easier to talk to a peer about interpersonal issues rather than an adult. Just like peer counselors, peer mediators undergo training to help them learn how to help others solve their problems.

Keeping confidential information that you hear can be hard if you are volunteering at your own school as a peer counselor or peer mediator. Other students often ask peer counselors and mediators for gossip. You must not participate, and you must keep the

Peer counselors are active listeners who give their complete attention to the person they are counseling. They can respond without judgment and help their peers to talk about their problems and help to solve them.

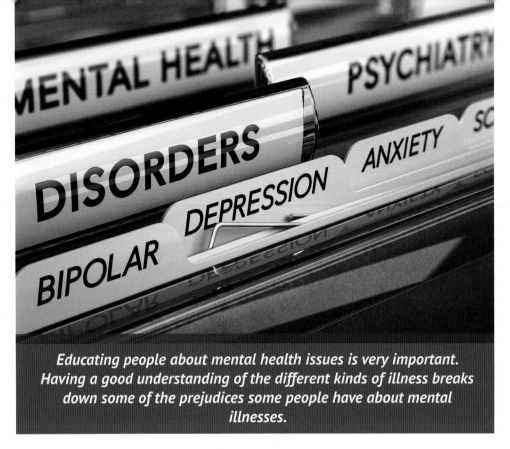

Educating people about mental health issues is very important. Having a good understanding of the different kinds of illness breaks down some of the prejudices some people have about mental illnesses.

information to yourself, as those who have sought your help are trusting you to keep their personal information private.

MENTAL HEALTH EDUCATION

If your school does not have a peer mentoring program, you may be able to work with your guidance office to educate others on the importance of mental health. This could involve presenting information to other students about depression, answering questions about mental health, or giving students tips for managing their anxiety during finals.

While the stigma of mental health is dissipating, many students still find it difficult to speak up when they are struggling with anxiety or depression. By providing correct information on these topics, you can let students know that they are not alone in their struggles and that it is Ok to ask for help. Educating others about how to take care of their mental health is an incredibly important job, and most schools do not have the resources to give students this information. Your guidance counselor may be able to help you give presentations in your school's health classes to educate other students.

A DAY IN THE LIFE: SCHOOL COUNSELOR

Many school counselors start their days by attending to any urgent matters that their students might be dealing with, such as a death in the family or a crisis at home. After that, school counselors have a variety of tasks to complete. They may meet with students who they have been counseling regularly. They may lead group therapy sessions for students who are dealing with similar issues, such as anxiety or dealing with parents who are going through a divorce.

School counselors often teach lessons in health classes about mental health. They also meet with parents and students together, talk with students about their college choices, administer standardized testing, and talk with teachers who are concerned about certain students. While most school counselors have a very full plate, they always put the needs of their students first.

CRISIS TEXT LINE VOLUNTEER

Watch this video to learn more about how texting someone through a crisis works

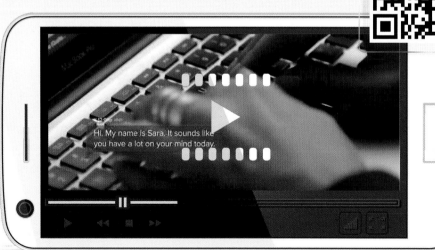

TEXT-DEPENDENT QUESTIONS

1. How old do you usually have to be to volunteer to help those with mental illness?

2. How much money does it cost to train a crisis text line volunteer?

3. What is peer counseling?

RESEARCH PROJECT

Choose one of the volunteer opportunities mentioned in this chapter, and research the pros and cons of this opportunity. Based on what you learn, do you think this opportunity would be good for you?

MENTAL HEALTH BILL OF RIGHTS—MARCH 1997

In 1997, nine psychology organizations came together to create the Mental Health Bill of Rights for patients. Among these organizations were the American Psychological Association, the American Psychiatric Association, the American Family Therapy Academy, and the American Psychiatric Nurses Association. This bill outlines the standard of care for mental health patients.

Professionals in this area of health care were frustrated because they were dedicating their careers to helping mental health patients, but they were seeing a large number of patients not getting the help they needed. Sometimes this was due to other medical professionals, and sometimes it was because insurance companies were putting other priorities ahead of mental health care. The underlying principles of the Mental Health Bill of Rights are that mental health patients need to be participants in their care. This means that if they are capable, they have the final say in medications, treatments, and inpatient hospital stays. Patients get to choose who gets to visit them and how often they are able to visit. Patients are able to request new doctors, medication changes, and new group therapy sessions as they see fit. Not only does this increase the rate of treatment success, it also helps patients gain confidence and a sense of control over their lives that they may have felt was lost due to mental illness.

WORDS TO UNDERSTAND

abnormal psychology: the study of mental illness and abnormal behavior in the field of psychology

direct-care: helping individuals with their activities of daily living, such as getting to and from work, eating, bathing, and cleaning

ethics: the study of morality, or right and wrong

sobriety: a period of time spent without using alcohol or drugs

CHAPTER 4

Education, Training, and Qualifications

CAREERS IN THE MENTAL HEALTH FIELD

If you want to work with people who are suffering from mental illness, it's key that you undergo education and training so that you can be an effective listener with a solid understanding of mental health issues and treatments. There are opportunities in the mental health field for professionals at all education levels. Many people work in the field while pursuing their degree. This is helpful for two reasons:

- It allows the student to gain firsthand experience, which is helpful both in the classroom and when looking for jobs later on.
- It allows the student to earn money to put toward tuition, lessening the amount of loans needed to cover the cost of higher education.

High school students who are considering a career in mental health have to make many important decisions to ensure that they end up taking the correct education and training to realize their goals.

No matter what level of education mental health workers have, it's important that they never stop learning. Information in the field of psychology is constantly changing as scientists and researchers learn more about the brain, behavior, and mental illness. Jobs in the mental health field frequently require employees to participate in continuing education classes, even if they already have a graduate degree. Typically, employers pay for their employees to take continuing education classes.

HIGH SCHOOL LEVEL

There are some jobs working with the mentally ill population that are attainable with a high school diploma. Most of these jobs are **direct-care** jobs, such as being a group home counselor. Some organizations will allow people who have a high school diploma to work while they are pursuing their bachelor's degree, and sometimes this type of work can count as college credit. If you're interested in doing this, it's a good idea to talk to your college advisor to find out if this is a possibility for you.

BACHELOR'S DEGREE LEVEL

If you're interested in pursuing mental health opportunities at the bachelor's degree level, you probably should major in psychology, sociology, or social work in college. In class, you'll learn about the history of psychology, famous psychological experiments, how psychological research is conducted, **ethics** in psychology, different types of mental illness, treatments for mental illness, and how the field of psychology is changing.

While at college, you'll be able to choose a focus area within the psychology field. If you're interested in working with children, you should probably concentrate on child development or education. If research is where you want to work, you'll want to look for classes on research methods and statistics. And if you want to become a mental health therapist, **abnormal psychology** and psychological treatment classes would be necessary.

There are many counseling positions that require a bachelor's degree. Addiction counselors, mental health nurses, and some youth counselors have bachelor's degrees. Organizations that employ people with bachelor's degrees often want their employees to have some level of experience before starting work. This can come in the form of volunteer experience.

After graduating from college, most professionals want to begin their careers right away. This is why it's a good idea to gain volunteer experience prior to college graduation.

One option for people who have bachelors degrees in psychology is to teach psychology

Most mental health professionals have to undergo education and training to qualify them for working in this field. In order to get qualified, they will require practical experience too.

A DAY IN THE LIFE: MENTAL HEALTH NURSE

When mental health nurses arrive at the hospital for a shift, the first thing that they do is make rounds to check on their patients. Doing rounds allows the nurse to update themselves on the status of the patients they'll be caring for, the medications the patients are taking, and any special needs they might have. Mental health nurses use this time to check in with patients—see how they're feeling and see who might need some extra attention that day. Then the nurses talk with doctors to update them on the needs of their patients.

Nurses administer direct care (such as medication, changing IV lines, and making sure a patient's needs are met), and they may talk with families to give them an update on the patient's condition. Often, nurses work twelve- to twenty-four-hour shifts two to three times a week and then have a few days off. This schedule can be challenging, but most nurses eventually adjust to having atypical working hours.

classes at high schools and/or community colleges. A lot of high schools are beginning to incorporate psychology classes into their curriculum. This is an excellent option for someone who is interested in eventually going to graduate school but does not want to go right away after college.

In order to teach psychology at a public school, a teaching certificate is required. Teaching certificate requirements are different from state to state. No certificate is required for teaching at a private school or at a college.

Some organizations also consider life experience to be a valuable piece of knowledge for counselors. Addiction centers have been known to hire former patients after they complete a certain number of years of **sobriety** and want to help others. The same is also true of eating disorder clinics. If you find yourself in this situation and want to help others who are headed down the same path, it's a good idea to get in touch with the counselors who helped you get on the right track.

POSTGRADUATE LEVEL

Many careers working with populations who have mental illnesses require a graduate degree. There are different levels of graduate degrees. The first level is a master's degree. This typically takes two years after graduating from college. Next is a doctoral degree, or a PhD. This typically takes eight years to complete after graduating from college with a bachelor's degree.

Becoming a psychiatrist is a little bit different from other careers in the mental health field, since a psychiatrist is a medical doctor with a specialty in psychiatry. Psychiatrists must go through full medical school training, just like any other doctor, to earn their MD. So in order to become a psychiatrist, medical school must be completed (four years), followed by the completion of a residency program (four additional years). During a residency, psychiatrists see patients under the supervision of a more experienced doctor. At least three of the four years of their residency are spent working with psychiatric patients.

After residency, psychiatrists take long tests called board exams. Some parts of the test are written. For other sections, they are observed while

Students who want to work in mental health at the highest level will usually have to study at the postgraduate level. Careers at this level usually need licensing from the state in order to legally practice.

conducting an appointment with an actual psychiatric patient. The observers are experienced psychiatrists who evaluate the skills of the person taking the test. After the test is passed, the psychiatrist is eligible to apply for certification from the state's licensing board. This certification lasts for ten years. Every ten years, psychiatrists must reapply for board certification.

Most counselors, therapists, and group home managers have completed at least some graduate-level work. Social workers also must have their master's degree before they are allowed to work. There are some jobs that will allow students who are working on their graduate degree to work while going to school. For other jobs, such as a school counselor or a private practice therapist, it's required that schooling is completed before work can begin.

Careers at this level need licensing from the state in order to legally practice. The requirements for licensing are different from state to state. Some states require the completion of specific graduate programs, while others require the passing of certain counseling tests. If you're interested in pursuing graduate work to work in the mental health field, it's a good idea to know what state you'd like to work in after you finish. That way you can make sure that the graduate program you choose is a good fit for the requirements of your state.

INTERNSHIPS

For graduate school programs, an internship is required in order to receive a diploma from a school and a

An internship is an important part of building a career in mental health. The time spent at the internship may be part of a qualification, and it provides valuable work experience, too.

Graduate students often find an internship quite challenging. While the internship is progressing, students have the added workload of managing their studies and a full-time job.

license from the state governing board. There are usually two parts to an internship: a practicum, in which the student observes a licensed professional, and an actual internship, during which the student practices in their career field while being supervised by a licensed professional. These two portions of internship do not necessarily need to happen in the same field. For example, if a student is interested in working in both schools and with families, they may do a part of their internship with a school counselor and another part with a family therapist. It is possible to find paid internships. Graduate school advisors can help students look for these if this if necessary.

Graduate students frequently find it challenging to manage classwork, a full-time job, and an internship. While this can be a very difficult time to find balance in life, it's important to remember that it will not last forever. Most professionals in the medical field go through a time in their training when they are extremely busy.

While completing an internship is important to get practice using the skills learned in graduate classes, it's also necessary to complete coursework. Graduate students often write case studies on the patients they work with during their internship, and these cases are presented to their graduate class for discussion. This may seem like a breach of the HIPAA policy, but this is permitted when identifying details (such as the person's name or the names of their family members) are changed.

DO COUNSELORS NEED COUNSELING?

Yes! Helping people work through their problems can be stressful, and a lot of professionals who work in the mental health field see a counselor or psychologist to help them deal with the stresses they have in their careers. It's ok for mental health professionals to talk about their jobs to their counselor, as their counselor is also strictly bound to confidentiality.

Mental health professionals often care deeply for their patients, and it's vital for their own mental health that they have a way to let go of the stress of the workday.

WHAT'S IT LIKE TO BE A SOCIAL WORKER?

Find out about the role that social workers play when helping people with mental health illnesses

TEXT-DEPENDENT QUESTIONS

1. How long does a psychiatrist have to go to school?

2. What jobs are available in the mental health field for people who have a bachelor's degree?

3. Why is it important to get volunteer experience before graduating college?

RESEARCH PROJECT

Research a psychology program at a local college or university. Find out what classes are required to graduate from the major, whether an internship is required, and what types of jobs students who graduate from the program typically get.

Milestone Moment

PUBLICATION OF SIMON LEVAY'S *GAY, STRAIGHT, AND THE REASON WHY: THE SCIENCE OF SEXUAL ORIENTATION*—1ST ED., 2010

In order to understand the importance of the first edition of this publication, one must first understand the history of how sexual orientation has been classified by psychologists over time. Many years ago, it was thought that being gay was a mental illness that needed to be treated or cured. This led to individuals feeling ashamed about their sexual identity. It also led to the general public believing that there was something wrong with gay people.

Thankfully, over time, this idea has changed. Psychologists now understand that a person's sexual orientation is not a choice, and

homosexuality is no longer considered a mental illness. The American Psychological Association has taken an official stance in support of same-sex marriage, and the organization has also publicly denounced sexual orientation conversion therapy.

Today, a person's sexual orientation is not considered a mental illness. People from the LGBTQ community are accepted into society without question.

WORDS TO UNDERSTAND

destigmatize: to remove associations of shame or disgrace

geriatrics: the branch of medicine or social science dealing with the health and care of the elderly

preventative: a type of medicine or treatment designed to keep the patient from harm

CHAPTER 5

Salaries, Job Outlook, and Work Satisfaction

MENTAL HEALTH COUNSELOR

A mental health counselor can work in a variety of settings, including a private practice, a self-owned business, a hospital, a rehabilitation center, and others. Many mental health counselors provide one-on-one talk therapy sessions in which they help clients identify and understand their problems and come up with potential solutions. People see mental health counselors when they need help working through a difficult area of their life. This can include relationship issues, family issues, job or school trouble, etc.

There are different types of mental health counselors. Cognitive behavioral therapy counselors help clients to change their thought patterns and behaviors. Humanistic counselors help sufferers learn to have

WHAT'S THE DIFFERENCE BETWEEN A PSYCHOLOGIST AND A PSYCHIATRIST?

Sometimes we hear these words used interchangeably, but they are not the same thing. Both professions require a doctoral degree and both deal with mental illness. The difference, however, lies in the fact that a psychiatrist is able to prescribe medication, while a psychologist is not. A psychologist is more likely to focus on talk therapy, while a psychiatrist may treat patients with a combination of talk therapy and medication. Psychologists and psychiatrists often work together to treat patients.

compassion for themselves. Solution-focused counselors provide short-term therapy that helps people figure out strategies to put an end to their problems.

No matter what style is predominantly practiced, most counselors use bits and pieces of different types of therapies to help their clients. Patients typically see mental health counselors for a few months at a time and then may begin seeing them again if problems reoccur. On average, mental health counselors earn $43,000 per year.

CLINICAL PSYCHOLOGIST

A clinical psychologist is a mental health doctor who usually works in a hospital or private practice. They diagnose, treat, and help people who are struggling with mental illness. A psychologist will utilize a variety of therapies to help their patients, but they do not prescribe medication.

Clinical psychologists frequently work closely with a patient's treatment team, which can include their other doctors, nurses, and counselors, to help create a plan to get their patient as healthy as possible. Clinical psychologists may also conduct and publish research on various psychology topics that pique their interest. Researching clinical psychologists can teach at universities or colleges and may also teach college- or graduate-level classes. On average, clinical psychologists earn $71,000 per year.

FAMILY THERAPIST

Family therapists meet with couples, parents and children, brothers and sisters, and other family unit members to help them conquer issues that they have with one another in a productive way. Families are often complicated, especially when parents are divorced and remarried, and when there are children involved. Family therapists can assist those in tough family situations work on communication, understanding, and empathy, resulting in a healthier family dynamic. On average, family therapists earn $49,000 per year.

RELATIONSHIP COUNSELOR

Relationship counselors help people who are in serious relationships or marriages to communicate better with one another. Sometimes couples seek this kind of counseling before they get married in order to make their relationship as strong as possible. Other people seek counseling when their relationship is struggling due to trust issues, a lack of communication, a betrayal, etc.

A clinical psychologist diagnoses and treats people with mental illnesses but they do not prescribe medication. Sometimes, they become involved in research at universities or colleges or teach.

Many couples have the false belief that seeking relationship counseling means that a relationship is in trouble, but most relationship counselors do not find this to be the case. Instead, participating in this type of counseling means that both parties care about their bond and are willing to put in the work and effort to improve the relationship. Couples who attend sessions with a relationship counselor generally find that their relationship improves.

Relationship counselors act as facilitators, helping couples to talk with each other about difficult subjects and moderating conversations when things become emotional or hard to talk about. Relationship counselors typically earn about $49,000 per year.

GROUP HOME COUNSELOR/MANAGER

Group homes are residences where people with mental illnesses live under the supervision of group home counselors and managers. Often, those living in group homes function as a family. They go to work together, they eat

Group home counselors provide day-to-day help for people with mental illnesses who live in a group home. Some counselors are trained to dispense medications to residents of the group home.

meals together, and they engage in recreational activities together, like exercise, watching movies, or going shopping. A group home counselor is someone who helps residents with these day-to-day activities.

Counselors may also undergo medication administration training, allowing them to dispense daily medications to group home residents. Sometimes counselors work a typical eight-hour day in the group home. Other times, they may stay for twenty-four hours or more. During these long shifts, counselors typically have a guest room in the group home in which they sleep and do work.

Group home managers function as both counselors and counselor supervisors. Managers are also typically in charge of creating the house budget, organizing schedules, and conducting one-on-one therapy

Psychiatrists are doctors who specialize in mental health. They usually work in hospitals alongside other health professionals.

sessions with residents. Group home counselors typically earn about $39,000 per year, while group home managers typically earn about $40,000 per year.

PSYCHIATRIST

Psychiatrists are medical mental health doctors who often wear many hats. They conduct one-on-one psychotherapy sessions with patients, work with general medical doctors to figure out medication doses for patients with mental illness, and are often part of a hospital's crisis team for patients and families in need. Psychiatrists are the doctors who actually diagnose patients with mental health issues. Psychologists and counselors often refer their patients to psychiatrists when they suspect that their patient may be suffering from mental illness.

About half of the psychiatrists in the United States work in private practice, and the other half work in hospitals. Psychiatrists often also do part-time work in drug detox and rehabilitation centers. It can be difficult work to treat someone who is recovering from substance abuse and dealing with mental illness at the same time, especially since some of the medications used to treat mental health conditions can be addictive.

An important part of a psychiatrist's job is to follow up with their patients and make sure their medication is continuing to work. There are many factors that can necessitate a change in medication, such as increasing age, weight gain or loss, variations in life stressors, changes in family situations, etc. A psychiatrist has to maintain a close relationship with their patients to ensure that their medication is continuing to do its job. In the United States, psychiatrists typically make about $175,000 per year.

MENTAL HEALTH SOCIAL WORKER

Social workers help individuals and families get the resources that they need to stay safe and healthy. Mental health social workers connect families with public and private programs to meet their mental health needs. If a family member is dealing with a mental health problem and the other members of the family are unsure where to turn, a mental health social worker can help them choose the best option while giving consideration to their financial situation.

Mental health social workers play an important role in the rehabilitation of people with mental illnesses. They work to support the patients and their families.

A mental health nurse spends a lot of time working closely with the patients in their care. Their work enables them to give doctors, psychologists, and psychiatrists insights into a patient's mental state.

Being a mental health social worker is not easy. Sometimes social workers need to remove children from unsafe homes, such as when a mentally ill parent is not able to care for their child. While this is difficult, social workers also work hard to reunite families that have been broken apart.

Most social workers make approximately $49,000 per year in the United States.

MENTAL HEALTH NURSE

Like all nurses, mental health nurses are responsible for the direct care of patients. Mental health nurses can work in a variety of settings, including hospitals, homes, nursing homes, mental hospitals, rehabilitation centers, and homeless shelters.

Mental health nurses are an important part of any successful mental health treatment team. Since nurses spend a lot of time working one-on-one with patients, they are able to give doctors, psychologists, and psychiatrists insights into a patient's behavior that the doctors might otherwise miss. Mental health nurses are often a patient's sounding board when it comes to complaints about their symptoms or care, and nurses have to be able to keep a positive attitude no matter what gets thrown at them throughout their shift. Mental health nurses make an average of $96,000 per year.

SUBSTANCE ABUSE COUNSELOR

Substance abuse counselors may work in detox centers, rehabilitation centers, halfway houses, inpatient/outpatient treatment centers, and hospitals. They are often the first people that patients meet when they decide to seek treatment for addiction. It's important for substance abuse counselors to be open, nonjudgmental, and reassuring for persons who are seeking help. Most facilities that employ substance abuse counselors are open twenty-four hours a day, seven days a week, so scheduling may be different from that of a typical job.

Substance abuse counselors conduct intake interviews with new patients, hold one-on-one counseling sessions, lead group therapy sessions, and may also do family therapy sessions with patients and their loved ones. They help patients come up with aftercare plans so that they can maintain their sobriety when they leave treatment.

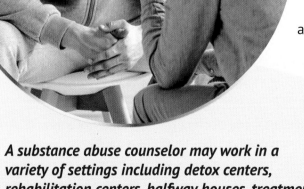

Substance abuse counselors are typically involved in follow-up care after patients have left the treatment facility and may also help them get set up with a sponsor—someone who has also struggled with addiction and checks in with them to ensure that they are maintaining a sober lifestyle. Substance abuse counselors usually make about $40,000 per year.

A substance abuse counselor may work in a variety of settings including detox centers, rehabilitation centers, halfway houses, treatment centers, and hospitals.

CRISIS COUNSELOR

A crisis counselor helps people when they feel they have nowhere else to turn. Crisis counselors often work with those who have been the victims of violent crime, such as arson, robbery, rape, or attempted murder. Crisis counselors are trained to recognize PTSD in victims and help them get the help that they need. These counselors usually provide immediate, short-term care after a person experiences a traumatic event. After that, crisis counselors refer victims to long-term care resources that fit their needs, such as a psychologist or mental health counselor.

Crisis counselors may also refer victims to a support group so that they can connect with others who have had similar experiences. Crisis counselors usually make about $38,000 per year.

CAREER COUNSELOR

Some people struggle to decide which career field to enter, and this is where a career counselor comes in. Career counselors help individuals choose a career field, decide on a specific position within that field, and then tailor their resume to apply for those jobs. Career counselors also help people practice interview skills and workplace etiquette.

Career counselors administer aptitude tests to their clients. These tests ask lots of questions about likes, dislikes, and special skills, and the results give the test taker different ideas about what careers are likely to be a good fit for them. Career counselors often work in high school and college counseling settings.

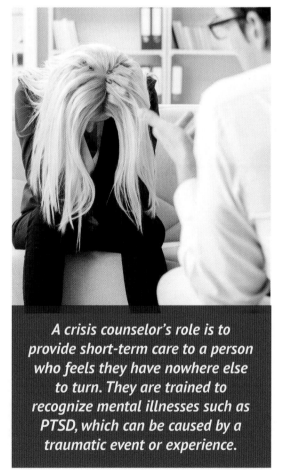

A crisis counselor's role is to provide short-term care to a person who feels they have nowhere else to turn. They are trained to recognize mental illnesses such as PTSD, which can be caused by a traumatic event or experience.

Many career counselors also work with folks who are struggling with mental illness. A career counselor can help someone with a mental illness practice the skills that are necessary to be successful in getting and keeping a job in their chosen career. Career counselors typically make about $56,000 per year.

SCHOOL COUNSELOR

School counselors help students deal with a range of problems, including mental illness, bullying, family issues, social problems, and disputes with teachers. School counselors can also assist students in choosing a career or college path. Some school counselors administer testing to identify gifted students.

In some schools, there are also group therapy programs for students who deal with similar issues. For example, it can be helpful for students who all suffer from depression to come together and learn about different coping strategies. School counselors usually make about $54,000 per year.

School counselors advise students on many matters including mental illnesses. They also help students find solutions to other problems that may affect their mental health.

MENTAL HEALTH

Research shows that in recent years, people who suffer from a mental illness are more likely to come forward to discuss their mental health with a trained professional than in the past.

JOB OUTLOOK

As mental health continues to be **destigmatized** in the United States, the need for mental health workers grows larger each year. It's expected that openings for psychologists will increase by as much as 19 percent in the coming ten years.

As people become more open to discussing mental health, more individuals recognize that they may need the help of a trained professional to deal with their psychological needs. This means that the demand for appointments with counselors and psychologists continues to grow.

However, if the demand for **preventative** mental health care continues to increase, it is likely that the need for crisis counselors, inpatient facility mental health workers, and drug and alcohol counselors will decrease. When people are able to deal with their mental health issues before they are in a crisis situation, it makes it more likely that they will be able to manage their illness with medication and therapy rather than finding their way into more extreme, less desirable situations.

There are a few areas in the mental health field that are growing more rapidly than others. In the coming years, it's expected that the need for psychiatrists will grow, especially for psychiatrists who specialize in the areas of **geriatrics** and child psychology.

WORK SATISFACTION

Many mental health professionals find their careers rewarding, but there are also difficulties to working with those who are struggling with mental illness. Careers in the mental health field are more stressful than other jobs in the medical field. Mental health professionals often work with patients who are more likely to become aggressive or suicidal than patients in other areas of medicine. In some hospitals, mental health professionals are viewed as less important than professionals who deal strictly with physical illnesses, even though mental health professionals often have the same amount of education, if not more, than general medicine doctors.

Mental health professionals are more prone to burnout than people in other careers in medicine. One of the reasons for burnout is a shortage of

Working in mental health can be tough at times, and as a consequence, mental health professionals are more likely to suffer from burnout than people in other careers in medicine.

professionals in the field. This often results in counselors, mental health nurses, psychologists, psychiatrists, and school counselors taking on more cases than they can reasonably handle. Those who choose to go into mental health often do so out of a desire to help others, so they are unlikely to say no when someone needs help. This can result in a large, unmanageable workload and a high level of stress.

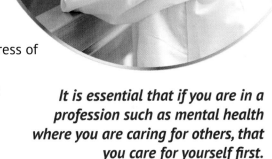

Mental health nurses have one of the highest rates of burnout of any career field. This is due to a few factors. Being a nurse in a mental health facility often means dealing with tough patients, day in and day out. The stress of the job means that these positions are constantly in high demand. But many psychiatric and psychology units in hospitals are short-staffed when it comes to nurses, requiring the nurses that they hire to work more hours than they would in another area of the hospital.

It is essential that if you are in a profession such as mental health where you are caring for others, that you care for yourself first.

Those who work with patients with mental illness must prioritize their own self-care. Studies show that mental health professionals who make it a point to take care of themselves have better job performance and are better able to help their patients. Generally, people who go into psychology are giving, often to the point of putting others ahead of themselves. While this is admirable, it's important to remember that it's not possible to care for others if you do not care for yourself first.

A DAY IN THE LIFE: PSYCHIATRIST

What's it like to be a psychiatrist? A psychiatrist is a medical doctor, and most of their day is typically spent meeting with patients and/or their families. During these appointments, psychiatrists talk with patients to see how their medication is working and assess their symptoms and then use that information to decide if medication changes are necessary. Psychiatrists are often part of a patient's larger treatment team, and their day might include meeting with a patient's full treatment team to help devise a course of action for that patient.

WHAT IS IT LIKE TO BE A PSYCHOLOGIST?

Find out how psychologists look for ways to help people engage in healthy behavior

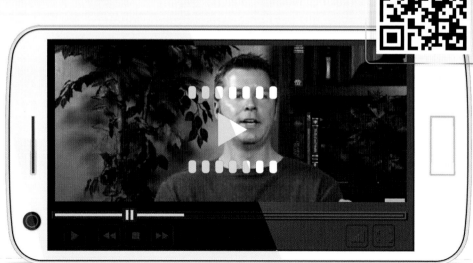

TEXT-DEPENDENT QUESTIONS

1. Which careers listed in this chapter make the highest salary?

2. What's one of the day-to-day tasks of a mental health nurse?

3. Are careers in psychology expected to increase or decrease over the next ten years?

RESEARCH PROJECT

Choose one of the careers discussed in this chapter, and interview someone in that field. Does this career sound like something you might want to pursue? Create a list of pros and cons of going into this career.

SERIES GLOSSARY OF KEY TERMS

abuse: Wrong or unfair treatment or use.

academic: Of or relating to schools and education.

advancement: Progression to a higher stage of development.

anxiety: Fear or nervousness about what might happen.

apprentice: A person who learns a job or skill by working for a fixed period of time for someone who is very good at that job or skill.

culture: A way of thinking, behaving, or working that exists in a place or organization (such as a business.)

donation: The making of an especially charitable gift.

empathy: The ability to understand and share the feelings of others.

endangered species: A specific type of plant or animal that is likely to become extinct in the near future.

ethics: The study of morality, or right and wrong.

food security: Having reliable access to a steady source of nutritious food.

intern: A student or recent graduate in a special field of study (as medicine or teaching) who works for a period of time to gain practical experience.

mediation: Intervention between conflicting parties to promote reconciliation, settlement, or compromise.

nonprofit: A charitable organization that uses its money to help others, rather than to make financial gain, aka "profit."

ombudsman: A person who advocates for the needs and wants of an individual in a facility anonymously so that the individual receiving care can voice complaints without fear of consequences.

pediatrician: A doctor who specializes in the care of babies and children.

perpetrator: A person who commits a harmful or illegal act.

poverty: The state of one who lacks a usual or socially acceptable amount of money or material possessions.

retaliate: To do something bad to someone who has hurt you or treated you badly; to get revenge against someone.

salary: The amount of money you receive each year for the work you perform.

sanctuary: A place of refuge and protection.

stress: Something that causes strong feelings of worry or anxiety.

substance abuse: Excessive use of a drug (such as alcohol, narcotics, or cocaine); use of a drug without medical justification.

syndrome: A group of signs and symptoms that occur together and characterize a particular abnormality or condition.

therapist: A person trained in methods of treatment and rehabilitation other than the use of drugs or surgery.

ORGANIZATIONS TO CONTACT

Active Minds: 2001 S St., NW Suite 630, Washington, DC 20009.
Phone: (202) 332-9595
    Website: www.activeminds.org/

American Psychological Association (APA): 750 First St. NE, Washington,
DC 20002-4242. Phone: (202) 336-5500
    Website: www.apa.org

Anxiety and Depression Association of America (ADAA): 8701 Georgia
Ave., Suite #412 Silver Spring, MD 20910 Phone: (240) 485-1001
    Website: https://adaa.org

Brain & Behavior Research Foundation: 747 Third Ave., 33rd Floor
New York, NY 10017. Phone: (646) 681-4888
    Website: www.bbrfoundation.org

The Flawless Foundation: P.O. Box 32024
Palm Beach Gardens, FL 33420. Phone: (917) 501-6078
    Website: http://flawlessfoundation.org

International OCD Foundation: P.O. Box 961029, Boston, MA 02196.
Phone (617) 973-5801
    Website: https://iocdf.org/

Mental Health America: 500 Montgomery St., Suite 820
Alexandria, VA 22314. Phone: (703) 684-7722.
    Website: www.mentalhealthamerica.net

Substance Abuse and Mental Health Services Administration: 5600
Fishers Ln., Rockville, MD 20857. Phone: (877) 726-4727
    Website: www.samhsa.gov

INTERNET RESOURCES

www.apa.org
The official website of the American Psychological Association provides up-to-date information on the latest news, research, and discoveries in the field of psychology.

www.centeronaddiction.org
The Center on Addiction website provides information for individuals who are struggling with addiction, and counselors, and families of people who are struggling with addiction.

www.nbcc.org
The site for the National Board for Certified Counselors offers information and resources for students who are interested in starting the path toward becoming a counselor.

www.psychologytoday.com/us
The American website for *Psychology Today* magazine provides interesting resources, articles, and research for those who are interested in psychology.

www.schoolcounselor.org
The official website of the American School Counselor Association provides information on the latest research in school counseling, as well as information on how to become a school counselor.

FURTHER READING

Kandel, Eric R. *The Disordered Mind: What Unusual Brains Tell Us about Ourselves*. New York: Farrar, Straus, and Giroux, 2018.

Korb, Alex, and Daniel Siegel. *The Upward Spiral: Using Neuroscience to Reverse the Course of Depression, One Small Change at a Time*. Oakland, CA: New Harbinger, 2015.

Perry, Bruce, and Maia Szalavitz. *The Boy Who Was Raised as a Dog: And Other Stories from a Child Psychiatrist's Notebook— What Traumatized Children Can Teach Us About Loss, Love, and Healing*. New York: Basic Books, 2017.

Phillips, Adam. *Becoming Freud: The Making of a Psychoanalyst*. New Haven, CT: Yale University Press, 2016.

Powers, Ron. *No One Cares about Crazy People: The Chaos and Heartbreak of Mental Health in America*. New York: Hachette Books, 2017.

INDEX

AUTHOR'S BIOGRAPHY

AMANDA TURNER lives in Dayton, Ohio, with her husband, son, dog, and cat. A former middle school teacher, she now enjoys traveling the country with her family wherever the Air Force chooses to send them! Amanda earned her BA in psychology from Penn State University and her MEd in school and mental health counseling from the University of Pennsylvania.

CREDITS

VIDEOS
Page 32 Eugene Hwang: http://x-qr.net/1Gpt
page 46 WebMD: http://x-qr.net/1GpV
page 56 Student Edge: http://x-qr.net/1H67
page 72 eHow: http://x-qr.net/1GeZ